EASYWAY GUIDES

A Guide to Handling Bereavement

The Easyway
Adrian Lewis

Easyway Guides

Easyway Guides
Brighton BN7 2SH

© Straightforward Publishing 2011

British Library Cataloguing in Publication Data. A catalogue record is available for this book from the British Library.

ISBN 9781847161857

Printed and bound by GN Digital Books Essex

Cover design by Bookworks Islington

Whilst every effort has been taken to ensure that the information contained in this book was accurate at the time of going to print, the publisher and the author cannot accept any liability for any inaccuracies contained within or for changes in legislation since writing the book.

A Guide to Handling Bereavement

CONTENTS

Introduction

Death is an unpleasant reality and one that many people avoid thinking about. However, on the death of a person who is close there are very necessary actions that need to be taken. This book is an attempt to enlighten the reader as to the practical steps that need to be taken after the death of a person. Each step is outlined along with the role of the funeral director and the role of the church and crematoria after death.

The role of the coroner is outlined and also the doctor, registrar, clergymen and cemetery and crematorium officials. This book does not dwell in depth on bereavement counseling, as this is a separate area and warrants a book on its own. It does, however, outline the process of grief and discuss aspects of this and offers advice in a limited way. The book is very much a practical guide and has been written in the hope that people may benefit from it at this difficult time.

There is a section on non-Christian burial in the recognition that the United Kingdom is a diverse multi-racial society and different traditions apply to different cultures.

There is also a section on wills and probate, as dealing with an estate after death can be very complex and time consuming, particularly if there is no will. Finally, there is a list of useful addresses at the end of the book.

11

1

Death and the Registration Of Death

If you suspect a person is dead, the first thing that you should do is to tell a doctor. There may be some doubt as to whether the person has died. In all cases, call a doctor or phone the ambulance service. Ask whether the doctor is going to attend. If the death of a person has been expected, then it may not be immediately necessary for a doctor to attend late at night, the next morning will do.

If the doctor does not intend to come, for reasons made very clear, then you need to ask for permission for a funeral director to remove the body. If a decision has been made that the funeral will be a cremation, the doctor will need to know as special papers will need to be drawn up which will involve an inspection, separately, by two doctors. If you intend to keep a body at home prior to such an inspection, which can be carried out in a funeral parlour, then it will be necessary to keep the room at a cool temperature.

Laying out a body

This is the first stage in preparing a body for burial or cremation.

If carried out by a funeral director it is termed last offices the "first office", denoting either the first or last contact. The body is washed and tidied up, eyelids closed and jaw closed. Hair is tidied, arms and legs And Hair usually grows for sometime after a death so therefore will need shaving. If a funeral director is laying out a body then a gown or everyday clothes will be applied.

Although laying out and general preparation can be carried out at home, and a funeral director can also provide a service in the home it is usual to allow the body to be taken away to a funeral parlor. An occurrence after death is Rigor Mortis, which is a stiffening of the muscles. This begins normally six hours after death and takes effect all over the body within 24 hours, after which it usually begins to wear off. In addition, about half an hour after death parts of the dead persons skin will begin to show dark patches. This activity is called Hypostasis and is due to settlement of the blood in the body due to gravity.

Police involvement

In certain circumstances it may be necessary to call the police if a persons death is not due to natural circumstances. It could be that a death is the result of murder or other suspicious circumstance. It is very important not to touch anything in the room as you may disturb vital evidence. The police will take statements from anyone with the person before death. There may at times be difficulty in identifying a dead body and the police have a specific procedure in this case.

Certificate of cause of death

In the United Kingdom, every death must be recorded in the local registrar's office within five days. The Registrar will always require a certificate as to the cause of death. If the cause of death is known then the doctor attending on death will provide the certificate, which states cause, when last seen alive and whether or not any doctor has seen the body since death occurred. This certificate will be given to the family. No charge is usually made.

If the doctor concerned is uncertain about the cause of death or has not seen the body for 14 days after death then a certificate cannot be issued and the coroners office is informed. The body is taken to the coroner's mortuary and a post mortem may or may not be carried out.

The coroner

A Coroner is a qualified doctor or solicitor and is paid by the local authority. The coroner is independent of both local and central government and is responsible only to the Crown. The coroner is assisted by the coroner's officer, usually a police officer. The coroner's office has contact with the public.

When a death occurs which is not due to natural causes it must be reported to the coroner. If the deceased died of natural causes but was not seen by a doctor for a significant time before death or after death then the coroner must be reported. The deceased

15

person's doctor will be contacted and cause of death and circumstances ascertained. If satisfied the coroner will cease involvement and issue a certificate and the family can then register the death normally. In any cases where the doctor is uncertain as to the cause of the death then the coroner must be notified. Death resulting from industrial disease, which has given rise to compensation, must be reported to the coroner. In addition, death arising from military service must be reported, in some but not all cases. Other circumstances in which death has arisen which must be reported are:

- If the death was suspicious

- Was sudden or unexplained

- Due to neglect, i.e., poisoning, drugs etc
- Caused directly or indirectly by accident

- Suicide

- In prison or police custody

Another situation is during surgery or before recovering from the effects of anesthetic.

When a death is reported to a coroner, and an investigation is decided upon then a death cannot be registered until enquiries are complete. There will usually be a post mortem. If death is shown to be from natural causes then the family will be notified and the death can be registered normally.

The family of the deceased do not have to be consulted or asked about carrying out a post mortem. If the law requires it then the coroner has to proceed. However, if a family or individual objects they can register that objection with the coroner who has to listen and give reasons for a post mortem. If there are still objections there is the right of appeal to the High Court. This will delay disposal of the body. The coroner has no duty to inform the next of kin about findings of a post mortem. After the post mortem, and a coroner's report made to the relevant authorities, the body becomes the responsibility of the family.

The coroner is obliged to hold an inquest into every violent and unnatural death and also death whilst in prison. The inquest is open to the public and can take the form of a trial, with witnesses called. The office of the coroner is a powerful office and the intention is to ensure that death was natural and not due to violent or other unnatural means. After the inquest is over then the death can be registered in the normal way.

Information concerning death, including the handing in of a certificate or the informing of the registrar of an extended period without certificate due to post mortem or other examination, can be given at any registrar's office (In England and Wales). This will then be passed on to the appropriate district or sub office.

17

Registration of death

As stated, in England, Wales and Northern Ireland a death should be registered within five days of occurrence. Registration can be delayed for up to another nine days if the registrar receives written confirmation that a doctor has signed a medical certificate of cause of death. The medical certificate must be presented at the register office in the sub-district where the death occurred. The person registering death must decide how many copies of the death certificate is needed and pay for them at the office. Payment can be by cheque, or credit card id ordering online or by telephone. The cost currently (2011) is £9.25 standard service or £23.40 priority service. If the death certificate is to be sent to someone else then the details must be given to the registrar. It is possible at this stage for what is known as the "Green certificate" authorising burial or cremation to be sent to the funeral director carrying out the funeral arrangements.

Names addresses and phone numbers of local registrars can be found in doctors surgeries, libraries etc.

Registrar's requirements

Registrar's information is contained on a part of a medical certificate issued by the doctor. This part is entitled "notice to informant" and lists:

- The date and place of death

- The full name, including maiden name if appropriate of the deceased

- Date of birth

- Occupation

- Occupation of the husband if deceased was a married woman or widow

- Address

- Whether deceased was in receipt of pension or allowance from public funds

If the deceased was married, the date of birth of the surviving partner

The form also states that the deceased's medical card should be given to the registrar. The other side of this particular form gives details of who is qualified to inform the registrar of a death. If the death occurs in a house or any other public building, the following can inform a registrar of a death:

- A relative of the deceased who was present at the death

- A relative who was present during the last illness

- A relative of the deceased who was not present at the death or during the last illness but who lives in the district or sub-district where the death occurred

- A person who is not a relative but who was present at the time of death

- The occupier of the building where the death occurred, if aware of the details of death

- Any inmate of the building where the death occurred, if aware of the details of death

- The person causing the disposal of the body, meaning the person accepting responsibility for arranging the funeral, but not the funeral director, who cannot register the death

The above are in order of preference. If a person has been found dead elsewhere, the following are qualified to register the death:

- Any relative of the dead person able to provide the registrar with the required details

- Any person present at time of death

- The person who found the body

- The person in charge of the body (which will be the police if the body cannot be identified)

- The person accepting responsibility for arranging the funeral

Only a person qualified under the law can inform the registrar of the death. If the registrar considers that the cause of death supplied on the medical certificate is inadequate, or the death should have been reported to the coroner, the registrar must inform the coroner and wait for written authority to proceed before continuing with registration.

In cases where a coroner's inquest has been held, the coroner will act as the person informing death.

Registering a stillbirth

A stillborn child is a child born after the 24th week of pregnancy which did not at any time after being completely delivered from its mother breathe or show any signs of life. In the case of a stillbirth, both birth and death need to be registered. This is a single operation, which must be achieved within 42 days. Those qualified to register a stillbirth are:

- The mother

21

- The father if the child would have been legitimate had it been born alive

- The occupier of the house or other premises in which the stillbirth occurred

- A person who was present at the stillbirth or who found the stillborn child.

If a doctor was present during stillbirth that person can issue a certificate of stillbirth stating the cause of stillbirth and the duration of pregnancy. A certified midwife can also issue the certificate if a doctor was not present. If no doctor or midwife was present a parent or other qualified person can make a declaration on form 35, available from the registrar of births and deaths, saying that to the best of knowledge the child was stillborn. If there is any doubt as to whether the child was born alive or dead then details must be given to the coroner who may then order a post mortem or inquest into the death, following which a certificate can be issued.

Loss of foetus within 24 weeks is not considered to be a stillbirth but is categorised as a miscarriage. If the mother was in hospital at the time of the miscarriage, the hospital may offer to dispose of the remains, or to arrange for disposal. But if the parent(s) would like these buried or cremated in the usual way, it should be possible to arrange this with a cemetery or crematorium, provided a medical certificate is completed.

A lot of funeral directors will give their services free of charge on such occasions, although there may be a fee for crematoria that is incurred on behalf of clients.

Some hospitals offer reverent disposal of stillborn and miscarried children, which often involves a simple ceremony led by a chaplain. In such cases there may be no ashes for subsequent burial or scattering.

Death in a hospital

There is a slight difference to the procedures up to the time of registration if a death is in hospital. The relatives or next of kin are informed of the death by the hospital staff. If death was unexpected, for example, the result of an operation or accident, the coroner will be involved. Usually, all deaths occurring within 24 hours of an operation will be reported to the coroner. The coroner must by law be informed of all deaths under suspicious circumstances, or death due to medical mishap, industrial disease, violence, neglect, abortion or any kind of poisoning. If the person who died was not already an in-patient in a hospital then a member of the family may be asked to identify the body.

In cases where the coroner is involved it will not be possible to issue a medical certificate of the cause of death, but in other cases this is usually issued by the hospital doctor and given to the next of kin. If the person died before the hospital doctor had the chance to diagnose the cause, then the deceased patient's own doctor may be sometimes asked to issue the medical certificate. The deceased's possessions will have to be removed from the hospital, with a receipt needing to be signed on removal. If the medical certificate of the cause of death can be signed in the hospital then relatives will have to make arrangements to remove the body from the hospital mortuary. This will usually be the responsibility of the funeral director. Most funeral directors operate a 24-hour emergency service. However, there is no need to inform the director of a hospital death until the morning after death. If cremation is involved, the necessary forms will be filled in at the hospital. The body cannot be removed until this is done. There will be a charge for filling in the forms.

Carrying out a post mortem in a hospital

A hospital will sometimes wish to carry out a post mortem, not involving the coroner. This cannot be carried out without the permission of the next of kin. In cases where a coroner is involved permission is not required. If a coroner orders a post mortem then this is legally required and cannot be prevented.

Results are not automatically given to relatives and a request for these may have to be made. The procedure for registering a death is the same as for a death outside a hospital. The registration however, must be within the district where the hospital is situated.

Where there are no relatives or others to meet the cost of the funeral then the health authority has the power to do so. There are usually arrangements with local funeral directors to provide a simple funeral for the deceased.

The donation of organs for transplantation

Organ transplants help to save the lives of several thousand people per year and some thought needs to be given as to the possibility of donating organs from the dead person. Organs must be removed as soon as possible after death to prevent deterioration, which renders them useless. No organ can be removed for transplantation until a person is declared brain dead, known as "stem" death. In order to determine brain stem death a number of stringent tests are carried out, the criteria of which are laid down by the Royal College of Surgeons.

A patient must be under 75 years of age for their major organs to be suitable for transplantation. The patient must be HIV negative and free from major infection. He or she must be of a compatible blood group to the planned recipient of the organs.

Organs that can be transplanted

Essentially, the organs intended for transplant must be in good order. For example, the lungs of a heavy smoker would be unsuitable.

The following are the most commonly used for transplantation:

Heart

Heart transplants are considered for those patients with severe cardiac failure who are considered unsuitable for heart surgery.

Kidney

Kidneys are viable for around 48 hours following retrieval from the donor.

Liver

Liver transplants are required for patients with congenital malformation of the liver, hepatic failure, chronic liver disease, some cases of cancer and inborn metabolic errors.

Heart and lung

This particular operation is carried out for people with an advanced primary lung disease, or a condition leading to this, or lung disease arising as a result of cardiac problems.

The pancreas

Pancreas transplants are used for patients with type 1 diabetes. This operation may be solely a pancreas transplant or can be done together with the kidneys.

Lungs

One or both lungs can be transplanted.

Cornea

Damage to the cornea is a major cause of blindness. Cornea grafting is one major solution to blindness. There is no age limit for corneal donation and corneas can be removed up to 24 hours after the heart has stopped beating. Relatives of patients not dying in a hospital who want to carry out their wishes should first of all consult the donors GP or the ophthalmic department of the local hospital.

Heart valves

These can be transplanted following removal from a donor up to 72 hours after death. There are other parts of the body, which can be transplanted including the skin, bone, connective tissue, major blood vessels, fettle cells and bone marrow. When deciding whether or not to donate organs, religious and other cultural considerations will play a significant part. For Christians, organ donation is considered acceptable to Roman Catholics and Protestants. Christian Scientists, on the other hand, object to all forms of transplants. Buddhists do not object neither does the Jewish faith, with the exception of some orthodox Jews. Mormons have no objection neither do Hindu and Sikh. Muslims tend towards prohibition of organ transplants.

The National Health Service Organ Donor Register

This register is a computer data base set up at the UK Transplant Support Service Authority (UKTSSA). All transplant coordinators have access to the register, and it can be checked each time a donor becomes available. Although relatives of donors are still asked for their permission to donate, the fact that details are on the register and there is a donor card carried, the decision is made easier by inclusion on the register. Any driving licence issued after 1993 may be marked on the back indicating willingness to donate organs. Anyone wishing to be entered onto the register can do so by post or using a form available from doctor's surgeries, chemists, libraries and other public places.

Donation of a body for medical uses

Some people wish their body to used for medical education or research after death. If this was the wish of the deceased then the next of kin or the executor should contact HM Inspector of Anatomy for details of the relevant anatomy school. This should be done immediately after death. Offering a body may not lead to it being accepted due to too many offers or the nature of the death or whether the coroner is involved or how far away the body is.

Donation of the brain for medical research

Brain donation is a separate issue altogether from Organ donation and cannot be included on the NHS register. The Parkinson'

Disease Society Brain Research Centre, which is part of the Institute of Neurology at the University College of London must be instructed to the effect that the donor wishes to donate the brain and potential donors must inform the society in advance or leave clear instructions that this should be done in the event of their death.

It will be the responsibility of the medical school to make arrangements and pay for the funeral. The school will make arrangements for a simple funeral unless the relatives indicate otherwise.

Registration in Scotland

In Scotland the medical certificate of the cause of death is very similar to that in England. The obligation to give a certificate rests on the doctor who attended the dead person during their last illness. If there was no certificate in attendance then any doctor can issue a certificate. In most cases the certificate is given to a relative who will then send or give it to the Registrar of Deaths in their area. If a medical certificate of cause of death cannot be given, the registrar can register the death but must report the matter to the Procurator Fiscal.

There are no coroners as such in Scotland and the duties of a coroner are carried out by a Procurator fiscal. This particular person is a law officer and comes under the jurisdiction of the Lord Advocate. The key functions of the procurator fiscal includes responsibility for the investigation of all unexpected deaths including those under suspicious circumstances. If he or she is satisfied with the doctor's medical certificate and any police evidence then no further action will usually be taken. If there is doubt then a medical surgeon will be asked to report.

In most cases, a post mortem is not carried out and the doctor certifies the cause of death after an external examination. In those situations where a post mortem is deemed necessary then permission is sought from the sheriff. Where there is a possibility of criminal proceedings connected to the death then two surgeons will usually carry out the post mortem.

Death whilst in legal custody or at work must be the subject of a public enquiry which will take the place of an inquest in England. If the death is by natural causes, then there may not be a public enquiry.

A public enquiry is held before the sheriff in the local sheriff court. The procurator fiscal examines the witnesses but it is the sheriff who determines the cause of death. When the enquiry is completed the procurator fiscal notifies the result of the findings to the registrar general. If the death has not already been registered then the registrar general lets the local registrar in the district in which the death occurred know of the death.

In Scotland the law requires that every death must be registered within eight days of death. The person qualified to act as an informant is any relative of the dead person, any person present at the death, the deceased executor or other representative, the occupier of the premises where the death took place, or any person having knowledge of the particulars to be registered.

The death may be registered in the office for the district in which the death occurred or in the office in the district where the deceased had resided before his or her death. The death of anyone visiting Scotland must be registered where the death took place.

Registering a stillbirth

A stillbirth in Scotland must be registered within 21 days. A doctor or midwife will usually issue a certificate or the person informing can fill in a form 7, issued by the local registrar. In all cases of doubt, the Procurator Fiscal will get involved. If the body is to be cremated then a certificate of stillbirth must be given by the doctor who was present at the confinement.

Death Certificates

As is the practice in England, the Registrar will issue free of charge a certificate of registration of death which can be used for National Insurance purposes. All other death certificates carry a fee. A list of fees for the various functions carried out by the registrar can be obtained from any registrar's office, as in England.

When someone dies abroad

When someone dies abroad, the death may seem more distressing because of the complications of being away from home and dealing with strangers, but you can get help from the British authorities in the UK and overseas.

Finding out about the death

If a close friend or relative dies while you are in the UK

If the death has been reported to the British Consulate in the country where the person died, they will ask the UK police to inform the next of kin. If you hear of the death from someone else, for example a tour operator, you should contact the Foreign and Commonwealth Office (FCO) on 020 7008 1500 (open 24 hours).

Consular staff in London will keep in touch with the family and the Consulate abroad until burial or cremation overseas or until the deceased has been brought back to the UK. They will also tell the British Consul of your wishes for the funeral and take details of who will be responsible for paying the costs involved, such as bringing the body back to the UK.

If the person dies while you are abroad with them

The British Consul will support you by offering practical advice and help with funeral arrangements and other formalities such as inquests. If the person died while on a package holiday, the tour operator will be able to contact funeral directors and British Consular staff for you.

Registering the death where the person died

You will need to register the death according to local regulations and get a death certificate. The local police, British Consul or tour guide can advise you on how to do this. You can also often register the death at the British Consulate as well. You don't have to do this, but if you do you will be given a UK Death Certificate and a record will be kept at the General registrar's Office 'Overseas' records in the UK. You will also be able to get a copy of the Death certificate later from the General Register Office or from the British Consul in the country concerned. It is not possible to register the death with the British authorities in Australia, Canada, New Zealand, Ireland, South Africa or Zimbabwe.

Documents that you will need to register the death

When registering the death, you should take information about yourself and the deceased including:
- Full name
- Date of birth
- Passport number

- Where and when the passport was issued
- Details of the next of kin, if you are not the closest relative

Bringing the body home

If you wish to bring the body back to the UK, British Consular staff will help by putting you in touch with the international funeral director. The body will need to be embalmed and placed in a zinc-lined coffin before it can be removed from the country. It may take some time to bring the body home, especially if a post-mortem examination is held. Before you can bring the body home you will need a certified English translation of the foreign death certificate form the country in which the person died, authorization to remove the deceased's body from the country and a certificate of embalming. The British Consul can help to arrange this documentation.

Funeral costs

If the deceased's funeral costs are covered by travel insurance, contact the insurance company straight away. They will then contact the funeral directors for you and make the necessary arrangements. If the costs are not covered then all the costs concerned, including repatriation of the body and possessions.

Arranging the funeral in the UK

You will need to take an authenticated translation of the death certificate to the register office in the area you intend to hold the funeral. The registrar will then issue a 'certificate of no liability to register'. This certificate is usually given to the funeral director to enable the funeral to go ahead. The certificate is not required if a coroner has issued a Certificate E for Cremation or an Order for Burial.

If you wish to have the body cremated you will need a Cremation Order (or a form E if there was a post mortem) before you start planning the funeral.

Having a funeral abroad

You can arrange for the burial or cremation in the country where the person died. The British Consulate can give you information about this.

Deaths in disasters abroad

If the deceased has been killed in a disaster abroad, natural or otherwise, ask the Foreign and Commonwealth Office for help. They will provide support and advice. The main enquiry number is 020 7008 1500. The deceased will need to be identified and you may be asked for information about them including a physical description, name and address of the person's UK doctor or dentist. The police may also need a photograph and/or finger print samples from the deceased's house. For more information go to:

www.direct.gov.uk/en/Governmentcitizensandrights/Death

Going to see someone who has died

If you choose to have the person who has died looked after at the undertaker, you may well want to visit them. Spending time with someone who has died isn't everyone's choice.

Visiting someone who has died gives you:

- Time to accept what has happened;

- Time to let go;

- Time to take in the fact that your world has changed;

- Time to say what you have to say;

- Time to see that person looking peaceful, not as they were when they had just died.

If you think that it is a difficult thing to do consider that people who do go to see someone after death are often the better for it.

If the body has been badly injured you can still go and visit. Your funeral director may be able to make the body presentable. If not arrange for the body to be covered except, say, for a hand. Or you can arrange for the coffin to be covered, you simply sit on it.

Now read the key points from Chapter one.

Key points from Chapter one.

- On discovering a person is dead, always call a doctor

- If the doctor cannot come, you must ask for permission for a Funeral Director to remove the body

- In certain circumstances, it may be necessary to call the police if the death was in suspicious circumstances

- In the United Kingdom, every death must be recorded in the coroners office within five days

- If a doctor will not issue a death certificate then the coroners office must be informed and there will be a post mortem

- In cases where an inquest has been held, the coroner will act as the person informing death

- In the case of a stillbirth the birth and death must be registered within 42 days

- A different procedure applies to hospital deaths

- The decision to donate of organs will be influenced by religious and other matters

2

Steps after Registration

If you need to make arrangements in relation to the dead person's estate then you will need to obtain several copies of the certified death certificate. The cost is minor, currently £9.25 (2011), changing in April of every year. You will find that a separate certificate is needed for application for probate, for dealing with banks and insurance company's etc. Before applying for the death certificate then you should estimate how many you are likely to need.

It is important that you notify the Department of Work and Pensions and any other relevant agency about the death as you will need to make arrangements about pensions etc. There may be a number of other benefits that you can claim after death, including help with funeral costs from the social fund. The funeral director may have a stock of the appropriate forms, which you must fill in.

In addition to copies of the death certificate, the registrar will provide another certificate, known as the green certificate to say that the death is now registered and a funeral can go ahead. The funeral director cannot proceed without it. If the coroner is or has been involved in the death then a different process takes place, which will be outlined a little later on. If a registrars certificate has been issued before registration then the deceased can be buried only. If it has been issued after registration then it can be cremated. The funeral director will forward the certificate either to the cemetery authority or to the vicar of the appropriate churchyard or to the office of the local crematorium.

Copies of a death certificate can be obtained at a later date from the superintendent registrar if more than one month has elapsed, or from the registrar if still relatively soon after the date of death.

Applications for certificates by post can be made to the general register office, see addresses at the rear of this book. In Northern Ireland it should be made to the Registrar General. There is a fee, again relatively minor and a stamped addressed envelope will be needed.

3

Taking Decisions about a Funeral

Understandably, those closest to the deceased wish to get the funeral over with as soon as is practically possible. This is a reaction to the death and to bury a person is to disassociate from the trauma of death, or at least from the first manifestations. However, it is important in all cases to ensure that a decent burial is arranged.

In some cases, the bereaved person will have left instructions in a will concerning burial. There is no strict legal obligation to go by the wishes of the deceased however although it is usual to do so. If no instructions were left then the burial arrangements will usually be arranged by the next of kin or an executor of a will. If no next of kin can be traced and there is no executor, the hospital will accept responsibility to arrange a minimum priced funeral. Although any capable person can organise a funeral, it is usual in times such as this to enlist the help of a funeral director.

A funeral director by another name is an undertaker. As with all professions, there are associations regulating the activities of funeral directors, The National Association of Funeral Directors, The Funeral Standards Council and the National Society of Allied and Independent Funeral Directors. You should make sure that a funeral director chosen by you belongs to one of the above associations. If you choose an unregistered firm then there may be no comeback in cases of future problems. The function of the funeral director is to assume complete responsibility for organising and supplying all that is needed for a funeral and also to provide as much care as is possible for relatives at this difficult time. Some funeral directors will also offer a bereavement counseling service. It is up to the deceased's family to organise a funeral and contact a director, not the executor of an estate, although in practice the executor will take on this function if requested.

A funeral director will provide a quote for a funeral and you should be clear about this at the outset. As with all services there are varying degrees of service at different prices. Insurance can be taken out for a funeral during an individual's lifetime and there are a number of so called friendly societies who offer plans. Any scheme that you invest in, as with all savings schemes has to be regulated and in the case of funeral plans the regulatory body is the National Association For pre-paid Funeral Plans.

If there is a problem with money, this should be discussed with the funeral director who can assist by encouraging you to apply for a grant from the benefits agency. Normally however, the cost of a funeral is paid for from the deceased's estate.

Costs of a funeral

The price of a funeral will consist of two elements, the fees that the director pays out on the clients behalf-doctors fees, cremation fees if appropriate, fees for the minister, burial fees, gravediggers, flowers and so on. These are the people who provide a service and must be paid. Then there is the fee charged by the funeral director, removal of the deceased, preparation and arrangements, use of the chapel of rest, the hearse and limousine and bearers and so on.

There is a usual minimum price for a funeral starting with a basic funeral for around £700 plus any disbursements, usually around £300-600 for a cremation and more for a burial due to the increase in activities necessary. As far as price goes, cremation is most certainly cheaper. The average cost is around £300 as opposed for around £400 for a burial. Fees for burials will vary according to the whereabouts of the cemetery. A Church of England Burial tends to be marginally cheaper than others but most graveyards have little burial space left, often involving a second internment in a grave. Some funeral directors will charge for a complete service, including coffin while others will make a separate charge for the choice of coffin required. Funeral director will be able to show clients a range of types of coffin. The material that a coffin is made from varies and will greatly affect the price. Basic coffins are made from chipboard laminated with plastic foil. More expensive coffins are made from solid wood, usually oak. There are other coffins, made from strong cardboard. However, it is always best to closely inspect the type of coffin you intend to purchase and ask questions about its durability.

Whether you buy a coffin for a cremation or for a burial will also have some bearing on the type that you buy as weaker coffins will normally suffice for cremation. Each coffin must be fitted with a nameplate of the deceased. The plate will also usually contain the age and date of death.

Associated costs

The overall cost of a funeral will consist of the funeral director own fees and those paid to other as disbursements. There may well be extra costs, which are not paid direct to the funeral director, or if paid cover anything extra such as long journeys in limousines, special services etc. Any funeral director should supply you with a breakdown of what a funeral will cost before the funeral. Funeral directors will always explain different charges and conditions in various areas so that you have an idea of costs. It may well be that you decide that you wish to eliminate certain parts of the service to keep cost down.

There is a fee currently for a Church of England Services £61 (check this as it may vary) for the service and £150 for a burial in the churchyard. These are liable to change and are for guidelines only. It is always necessary to ascertain the exact cost from the funeral director. Fees for burial in a municipal city cemetery are likely to be a lot more than this.

Overall, the total cost of a funeral is around £2,500, which includes cremation. Burial will be more than this. Like a lot of services, different areas of the country will charge different prices and it is best to be sure before agreeing to a particular funeral. In addition, like anything else the sky can be the limit depending on what you want.

Obtaining help with funeral costs

If a person is on low income and is in difficulties over funeral expenses there is help from the social fund administered by the Department of Work and Pensions, although such help is subject to rigid criteria. The applicant or applicants partner must be in receipt of one or more benefits, Income support, Income based Job seekers allowance, Pension Credit, Housing Benefit, Council Tax Benefit, Working Tax Credit where a Disability or Severe Disability element is included or Child Tax Credit which is at a higher rate than the family element.. This applies only to the person arranging the funeral. And the person applying for the benefit must be the one arranging the funeral, the next of kin or person described as the next of kin. The benefit is means tested, and if there are savings (check amounts) these will be taken into account when assessing the grant. If there is a close relative able to pay the costs of the funeral then an award will not usually be made. More details of the benefits available can be obtained from dwp.gov.uk which is the Department of Work and pensions website.

If money becomes available out of the deceased's estate then this will be used to pay back the funeral expenses provided by the social fund. The benefits agency form is the SF200 and the funeral director can also help with this.

The Social Fund Payment will make provision for up to £700 (2011/12) towards the funeral directors fees, which must encompass almost all the costs. In addition a cremation fee will be paid and the costs of certain doctors forms. Although other small payments are made for necessary expenses the money really only provides for a simple dignified funeral. Other extras, which may be desired, are not covered. See chapter 8 for more details of benefits available.

Some local authorities provide a municipal funeral service. The cost is very much less than the average local funeral and details can be obtained from your local authority. Those relatives of a member of the armed forces who die in service may be able to receive help with funeral costs from the Ministry of Defence. Where a person dies without relatives, or no one can be traced then the local authority where the person died, or hospital if appropriate, will arrange a simple funeral. Many hospitals maintain a funeral fund and local authorities usually have close links with funeral directors.

The burial

Anyone, whether Christian or not, whose address is within the ecclesiastical parish is, in theory at least, entitled to be buried within the parish churchyard, even if a death occurs away from the parish. Some churches have burial grounds away from the church, where parishioners have the right of burial. Ex-parishioners and non-parishioners with family graves in a parish area have a right to be buried within a particular parish. It is the local vicar or parish priest who will make the decision about burial and also how much to charge. In London, certain special rules exist, under the London local Authorities Act 2007, concerning burials. See key points.

Those who are resident within the local parish have to pay a fee to the local church for a funeral service in church and burial in a churchyard. There are fees payable for a funeral service in a church and these should be checked with the local church. These fees change on an annual basis and are decided by the church. If the church service is followed by burial in a municipal or private cemetery then the fee remains the same. There is a fee for a burial in a churchyard without having had a service beforehand. No fee is payable for the burial of a stillborn child or for the funeral or burial of an infant who died within one year of birth. If the ashes are to be buried in a churchyard following cremation there is a fee and if there is to be a further service following cremation then a fee will be payable. This fee does not apply if there is a simple service of committal. There are additional fees, such as grave diggers fees, this being up to £100. This can be more expensive if a funeral director provides the gravedigger.

A vicar will allot the site of a grave in a churchyard. The burial fee does not entitle anyone to the ownership of the grave or any rights of burial there. If you want the exclusive use of a particular plot in a graveyard, you must apply to the diocesan register to reserve a grave space. This is by the grant of a licence called a faculty. The freehold of the ground, in all circumstances belongs to the church. Normally it takes about six weeks for a faculty to be granted. A faculty must be applied for before death. It is too late after death.

Burial in cemeteries

Most cemeteries are non-denominational, and are run and managed by either a local authority or a privately owned company. Particular denominations own a few cemeteries in the U.K and burial places are restricted to members of that denomination. Some cemeteries will have a section of the ground consecrated by the Church of England, while the opening of new cemeteries is attended by a service of consecration for the whole area. The fee payable to a member of the Church of England Clergy for holding a ceremony is the same as that for a funeral service in a church. There will be no church fee.

Some cemeteries have ground dedicated to, or reserved for other specific religious groups, and a separate section of general ground.

In most cemeteries any type of religious service, or non-service at all, can be held. Many cemeteries have a chapel in which non-denominational services can be held. Some cemeteries will provide the services of a chaplain for burial services on a root basis. There is usually a choice of Church of England, Free Church or Roman Catholic.

Fees for burial in a cemetery vary according to where it is and who owns it. Fees are usually displayed at the cemetery. It is necessary to make enquiries as to what the fees cover and to obtain an itemised estimate of cost. In most local authority cemeteries, a higher fee is required for those who are not resident within the area. These can be double or treble the normal fees.

Cemetery fees are divided into two parts: there is a charge for purchasing the exclusive rights of burial in a particular plot and an additional charge for internment. These charges will vary considerably. Most local authority cemeteries have an application form which the executor or next of kin is required to fill in. All fees must be paid before the funeral and all documents sent. Normally, as stated this will usually be dealt with by a funeral director.

Types of grave

There are different categories of grave in a cemetery. At the one end of the scale are graves without exclusive rights of burial. The person paying for a burial has no rights to say who else may be buried in the grave. The graves are given a number, marked by a number and usually it is not allowed to put up a plaque by the grave. In a few cemeteries, for a small fee a grave space can be reserved for a specific period of time from the date of payment. After this time it reverts to the cemetery.

In most cemeteries it is possible to buy the right to a specific plot for a period usually not exceeding 50 years. Obviously, this is more expensive than the other options. For a private grave, a deed of grant is given for which cemeteries make a small charge.

Another type of grave is what is known as the "lawn grave" in which a person has the right to exclusive burial, but can put up a simple headstone leaving the rest of the grave as grass. This grave is easier to maintain and a lot of modern cemeteries allow lawn graves only.

Other burial places

If you want to be buried in ground other than churchyard ground then the law stipulates that such burials be registered. The deeds to land, even freehold, may impose restrictions on use and enquiries should be made to local authority Environmental Health and Planning Departments. There is the right in certain circumstances to a burial at sea which will be discussed a little later. In addition, there is what is known as "woodland burial" where plots are made available in meadowland or other woodland No burial plaque or stone is normally permitted and the emphasis is on the maintenance of a natural environment.

Cremation

The majority of funerals involve the act of cremation rather than burial. As discussed earlier, cremation cannot take place until the correct certificates have been produced and the death registered. Four statutory forms have to be completed before cremation can take place; one by the next of kin or the executor, the others by three different doctors. Forms are issued by the crematorium.

Both funeral directors and doctors normally keep a supply. The first form, form A is an application for cremation and has to be completed by the next of kin or the executor and countersigned by a householder who knows that person personally. Forms B and C are on the same piece of paper and has to be completed by the doctor who attended the deceased during the last illness.

Form C is the confirmatory medical certificate, and must be completed by a doctor who has been a medical practitioner (registered) for five years or more in the United Kingdom.

Doctors must not be related to the deceased or work on the same ward if they are hospital workers. In other words, they should be independent of each other.

Form F is the fourth statutory document which has to be signed by the medical referee of the crematorium, stating that he or she is satisfied with the details on forms B and C, or the coroners certificate for cremation. The medical referee can prevent

51

cremation taking place and can order a post mortem to take place or refer the matter to the coroner. Relatives have no right to prevent this post mortem. If they do not want it to take place then they must bury the deceased instead.

When the coroner is involved and has ordered a post mortem, he or she will issue a certificate for cremation. Forms B and C are not required. When a death is reported to the coroner, he or she must be informed at the outset if the funeral is to involve cremation, so that the appropriate certificate can be issued. This is form E and will be supplied as a pink form to the relatives so that they may register and as a yellow form to the funeral director for submission to the crematorium.

If the body of a stillborn child is to be cremated, a special medical certificate has to be issued by a doctor who was present at the birth, or who examined the body after birth. No second medical certificate is required, but the medical referee still has to complete form F. Many crematoria do not charge for the cremation of stillborn children, or infants up to the age of one year.

Fees for cremation

Fees include the charges made by the crematorium, the fees for the doctor's certificates and usually a standard fee for the minister who takes the service. An organist also needs to be paid in addition to other costs. The funeral director will usually pay all fees and charge accordingly. Crematorium fees can vary from

£500-£600 (2011/2012), with extra fees for those who did not reside in the district of cremation. Doctors who prepare initial forms will usually charge a minimum fee which rises each year. On occasions, when death has occurred in a hospital, the hospital will wish to carry out a post mortem to improve their knowledge of the patient's condition. The consent of relatives must be given and if so, form C will not be required-providing the post mortem was carried out by a pathologist of not less than five years standing and the result known by the doctor who completed form B. Only one fee will be charged, unless the pathologist was less than five years standing, in which case another doctor must complete form C and the full fee will be charged.

Most crematoria charge reduced fees for children up to school leaving age. You should check the above fees as they change subject to notice.

The majority of crematoria are run by local authorities, although private crematoria do exist. Each has its scale of fees and offers a brochure of services and fees, usually having an open day for the public, usually Sunday, as crematoria are open only from Monday to Friday, with occasional Saturdays.

Services in a crematorium

Charges for a crematorium will normally include the chapel, whether or not it is used. Chapels are non-denominational, catering for a variety of religions. Music can be chosen by the relatives. If they wish, relatives can opt for a non-religious funeral. Funeral directors can usually refer you to someone who can organise this.

Cremations and memorials

Most crematoriums will have various forms of memorial. There will be a book of remembrance in which the name of the deceased can be inscribed. Other memorials involve wall plaques, memorial flowers or rose bushes. There will usually be an extra charge for this. Some more sophisticated crematoria have extensive means of remembrance in their landscaped gardens. Again, there will be a charge for this.

Remains

Cremated remains or ashes of the deceased may be scattered in the grounds of the crematorium, taken away to be scattered elsewhere or buried in a local churchyard or cemetery. The crematorium will not usually charge a fee for scattering ashes after a funeral. However, a fee will be charged if ashes are stored and scattered later. There will usually be a fee if the ashes are to be scattered in a crematorium to the one where the funeral took place.

There is a Church of England Charge for the burial of ashes in a churchyard. This is around £110, at current prices, increasing annually. However, these prices should be checked with the relevant church.

A useful leaflet concerning cremation, "Questions People ask" is available from some local crematoria.

Events before a funeral

Most funeral directors maintain a 24-hour service. If death occurs at home or in a nursing home, two funeral directors will arrive fairly rapidly and take the body to the mortuary. It is rare for a body to remain at home between death and the funeral although is possible if requested by relatives.

It is recommended that a funeral director be approached as soon as is possible after a death.

When a body is taken by a funeral director then it will lie in a chapel of rest, where the body will lie in a coffin before the funeral. Laying out of a body will almost always take place in the funeral director mortuary. Arrangements need to be made about any jewelry and also clothes, as the funeral director can supply a gown if necessary.

If a person dies in hospital the body is usually taken to the hospital mortuary-although a number of hospitals normally subcontract mortuary facilities to a funeral director. When a body is removed by a funeral director it will lie until cremation papers have been completed. If a coroner has decided that a post mortem is necessary then the body will be taken to the mortuary in preparation.

When a body is kept in a chapel of rest, relatives and friends can go to see it before the funeral. Sometimes, there will be an extra charge to see the body at evenings and weekends.

Some larger firms of funeral directors also have chapels for private prayer, in which a religious service can be held at the beginning of the funeral before the cortege leaves for the cemetery or crematorium.

Embalming a body

The process of embalming is intended to delay the process of decomposition of a body. The blood in a body is replaced with a preservative, normally a solution of formalin. This is similar to a blood transfusion. It is necessary to embalm a body if it is returned to a private house to await a funeral or if the funeral is to be held more than five days after a death and cannot be put into cold storage.

Before a body can be embalmed, a doctor must have completed the medical certificate of the cause of death and the death registered. When cremation is involved, forms B and C must also have been completed.

If the coroner is involved then embalming cannot take place unless permission has been obtained. Embalmers are qualified and no one else other than a qualified person should be used.

The final arrangements before a funeral

The funeral director must have the registrar's disposal certificate before confirming the final arrangements. All of the functions connected with burial or cremation must have been completed and all fees paid.

The funeral director or a member of the family should ask whoever the family wishes to officiate at the service whether they can or are willing to do so, and at the allotted time or date. Services can be held in a church, churchyard, cemetery, crematorium chapel, village hall or any other suitable place. Funeral services can be held anywhere, with no particular form of licensing necessary.

Non-Church of England Funerals

Denominational burial grounds usually insist on their own form of service. For a practising Roman Catholic it is usual for a priest to say a requiem mass in the local parish church and for the priest to take the funeral service.

With Orthodox Jews, the body should be buried as soon as possible once the disposal certificate has been issued. If a man subscribes to a synagogue burial society, he or his wife and children will be buried free by the society in its cemetery. Orthodox Jews are never cremated, and embalming or bequeathing a body for medical purposes is never allowed. There are usually no flowers. The burial is simple. Reform non-orthodox Jews are not so rigid and permit cremation and flowers. If a Jew dies away from home it is the responsibility of the relatives to bring the body back at their own expense for the synagogue burial society to take over.

Non-religious services

There is no obligation to have a ceremony at a funeral. It is important to communicate this to the executor or person in charge if this is the case. If a body is to be buried in a churchyard without a religious ceremony, or by someone of another denomination, you should give at least 48 hours notice in writing. Usual fees are still applicable.

If the body is to be buried in a cemetery or cremated without religious ceremony, the funeral director or local authority should be informed. If there is to be no ceremony then usually a few members will attend the funeral and there will be a few minutes silence or with some music played.

Announcements of deaths are usually made in local papers. Sometimes, the national dailies will have an announcement. The address of the deceased should never be inserted in the obituary. A lot of houses have been broken into when a funeral takes place. The press notice should stipulate requirements for the giving of money to the deceased's favorite charity and also for flowers. The time and date and other arrangements for the funeral are included, and these details should be tailored to a families requirements. When a body is buried, flowers are normally left on a grave after it has been filled in. At a crematorium there will normally be restrictions as to where flowers can be placed.

The funeral

Although it was tradition for the cortege (procession) to travel from the house to the place of the funeral it is just as common, given the prominence of the funeral director, for the funeral to begin from the premises of the funeral director. If the funeral director provides cars for the relatives and friends of the deceased then he or she will organise and marshal the event and arrange departure.

The funeral director should have discussed all the details of the funeral with the family beforehand, and also arrange where people are to be taken after the funeral and also take care of other last minute arrangements. The funeral director may walk in front of the hearse as it leaves the deceased's house, and as it approaches the church or crematorium. This is both a mark of respect to the deceased and also a practical arrangement as he can direct the traffic. The coffin will be usually carried into the church or crematorium on the shoulders (or by handles on the coffin) of the funeral directors staff. Sometimes members of the family act as bearers. Occasionally, at the more formal funeral, pall-bearers walk alongside the coffin.

The burial

If a burial is preceded by a service in church, the coffin is taken into the church by the bearers and placed in front of the altar. In Roman Catholic churches the coffin is taken into the church before the funeral and remains there until the funeral takes place. After the service the bearers will take the coffin from the church to the churchyard or cemetery. If a burial is not preceded by a church service then the coffin is taken directly from the hearse to the cemetery. The coffin is lowered into the grave while the words of committal are said. A register of burial in the parish area is kept by the church. Copies can be obtained for a small fee.

When someone is buried in a Church of England churchyard, the family is responsible for the grave. Municipal and private cemeteries will employ grounds men to look after the common parts and also graves. Cemeteries often stipulate the provision of a simple grave in order to keep costs of maintenance down. A lot of churches have restrictions on the type of headstones and memorials used and it will be necessary to check with the church first before making any decisions.

Cremation

Traditionally, the funeral service prior to cremation was held in church, with the congregation travelling to the crematorium for a brief committal afterwards. It is an increasing practice for funeral services to be held entirely in a crematorium chapel. When the words of committal are spoken, the coffin passes out of site although some mourners prefer the coffin to remain until the last mourner has left the chapel. During the funeral service, the funeral directors staff will take flowers from the hearse and place them in the floral display area. The funeral director will take appropriate flowers to a hospital or nursing homes after the mourners have left. When the coffin is out of site it is taken to the committal room to await cremation. When the cremation process is complete the ashes are refined separately and placed in containers.

In the process of making arrangements for the cremation, the next of kin or executors of the deceased person's estate can ask to be present when the coffin is placed in the cremator. This is especially relevant for Hindu funerals where traditionally the next of kin would light the funeral pyre. Usually, only two people are allowed. Each crematorium will keep a register of cremations and again a copy can be obtained for a small fee. When making arrangements for a funeral, clients are asked what they would like to do with the ashes. While most ashes are scattered or buried in the crematorium grounds they can also be removed by next of kin to be scattered or buried elsewhere. When ashes are removed, the crematorium will normally provide a certificate confirming that the cremation has taken place. If ashes are to be scattered in the grounds of a different crematorium, there will be a fee of up to £30. There is no law regulating the disposal of ashes, they can be scattered anywhere, with consent from owners etc.

Burial in Scotland

In Scotland it is possible to purchase the exclusive rights to burial in a cemetery or churchyard (Kirkyard) plot. A grave is called a lair. Kirkyards are administered by the local district or islands council. Regulations and procedures for cremation are the same as in England and Wales.

Arranging a funeral without a funeral director

It is possible to arrange a funeral without using a funeral director. Most people will want a funeral director to take care of matters after death, due to grief and the wish to arrange matters quickly. However, some people prefer to arrange their own funeral.

If the coroner is not involved, a doctor's certificate as to the cause of death must be obtained and the death registered. The appropriate papers must be obtained and sent to the cemetery or crematorium with a fee. A date and time for the funeral must be arranged. A minister should be approached if they are to conduct the funeral. A coffin must be obtained along with the means of conveying the coffin to the funeral. If a burial is taking place a gravedigger must be hired

With cremation, the papers as outlined in this book must be obtained and a coffin and crematoria arrangements made. Coffins can be purchased from funeral supermarkets or from a funeral director. It is always highly advisable to purchase a coffin and not attempt to make one yourself. Biodegradable coffins can also be purchased for a fairly low price. These are normally made of cardboard. Details can be obtained from the natural death centre, address at the back of this book.

It is possible to arrange for a burial to take place on your own land-in a garden or a field. Planning permission is not necessary. However, there are other restrictions, one being the level of the water table and if this is likely to be affected. Other difficulties can arise, one being if a family or person decides to move house.

A Home Office Licence is required to exhume a body. As stated, although it is possible to carry out a funeral yourself, without a funeral director, it is not a common occurrence because of the amount of work involved. Many people decide to leave this to a funeral director.

At this point, it is worth outlining the practice of 'Green Funerals' as this is the choice of people who are either into environmentally friendly funerals or natural burials, where communing with nature is paramount.

Green funerals

A green funeral is an ethical choice and one which seeks not to harm the environment. It is also, for some, an aesthetic choice, which may appeal to those who have no particular environmental interests but rejects the traditional stuffy funeral in favour of an out doors, homespun, back to nature feel. It prefers an unspoilt landscape to that of a regimented ceremony.

An extreme green funeral

The elements of a real green funeral are as follows:

- Rejection of cremation
- Opts for burial in a site serving a conservation purpose
- Creates a site which is not visually definable as a burial ground
- Reviles embalming
- Requires a coffin or shroud locally made from natural, sustainable material
- Buries the body at a depth where it can decompose aerobically
- Rejects bought flowers, prefers garden flowers (if any)
- Forbids demarcation of the grave
- Forbids marking or personalizing of the grave with any sort of permanent memorial
- Forbids tending of the grave
- Discourages visits to the grave unless on foot or bike.

A real green funeral leaves no trace behind. However, there at present very few burial sites that meet the above criteria.

Most people who favour a natural burial want their decomposed body to nourish the plants and soil around it. Natural burial is a very personal form of recycling. Many like the idea of a tree planted on top of them. In a local authority cemetery, by law, no part of a coffin must be less than three feet below the surface except where soil conditions allow, in which case two feet will do. This is too deep to ensure truly vibrant aerobic decomposition. This law does not apply to private burial grounds. However, the Ministry of Justice is urging compliance.

Almost all natural burial grounds bury bodies at a depth where decomposition will be cold, slow and mostly anaerobic.

There are pluses and minuses when considering a green/natural burial as opposed to a conventional funeral. The Association of Natural Burial Grounds lists all green grounds in the UK. https://www.anbg.co.uk This site can also point the way to organizations that can give you more advice.

The Natural Death centre

The Natural Death Centre is a charity which campaigns for a change in social attitudes to death and dying. The philosophy of the NDC grew out of that of the natural childbirth movement. The NDC believes that tasking control; and keeping interventions by strangers to a minimum improves the quality of dying for the dying person and its impact on his or her carers. In the matter of caring for the dead it believes that taking control is therapeutic.

The NDC encourages and supports those who want to arrange environmentally friendly and inexpensive funerals, and it is behind the Association of Natural Burial grounds –anbg.co.uk.

A hands on approach to dealing with the dying and the dead strongly appeals to people of all sorts who know their own minds and like to do things their own way.

The NDC publishes The Natural Death Handbook, which is full of practical advice and personal stories. It operates a telephone helpline and offers free advice on all aspects of natural death and funerals.

Contact the NDC: naturaldeath.org, phone 0871 288 2098

Now read the key points from chapter three.

Key points from Chapter three

- In some cases the deceased person will have left instructions concerning his/her funeral. If no instructions were left the funeral will usually be arranged by the next of kin or the executor of the estate. If no next of kin can be traced and there is no executor then the hospital (if appropriate) will accept responsibility to arrange a minimum price funeral.

- A funeral director will usually carry out all the arrangements concerning the funeral

- A funeral will cost around one thousand pounds whilst cremation is significantly cheaper

- The Department of Work and Pensions can provide advice about help towards funeral for those on low incomes

- In London, under the London Local Authorities Act 2007, Councils can disturb human remains that have been buried for at least 75 years to deepen graves and allow more burials.

- Green funerals are the choice of people who want a more natural funeral.

4

Different Funerals

As Great Britain is a multi-racial society, obviously not all funeral and burials are Christian burials. Some space has to be given in a book like this to cover other funerals as they relate to different beliefs.

Muslim funerals

There are specific codes governing Muslim funerals. Muslims live by rigid moral codes and the Muslim funeral will reflect this.

Normally, Muslims will appoint one person to represent them in making arrangements for funerals. Muslims are always buried and never cremated. There is usually no coffin and the body is wrapped in a white sheet and buried within 24 hours of death in an unmarked grave, which must be raised up to 12 inches from the ground and can never be sat or walked upon.

Because of differences between the British tradition and Muslim requirements, one key difference being that a coffin is required in British cemeteries, special areas are sometimes designated by churches and other cemeteries. Because of the need to bury quickly, any requests for post mortem or organ donation are usually refused.

Muslims believe that the soul remains in the body sometime after death, and that the body remains conscious of pain. Bodies are therefore handled with care. Non-Muslims never handle bodies. Embalming is only usually allowed if a body is travelling over a long distance. The family will usually lay out a body and will place a head so that it is facing Mecca. Muslims must be buried facing Mecca. The family will normally perform all rites and blessings, together with the imam, the spiritual leader of the local mosque.

Hindu funerals

There are many Hindu deities, the three main being Brahma, the creator, Vishnu, the Preserver and Shiva, the Destroyer. Hindu belief in reincarnation means that most individuals face death in the hope of achieving a better life next time. Death is therefore relatively insignificant by comparison.

Hindus are always cremated and never buried. Most Hindus bring their dead into a chapel of rest and candles are lit. There are not normally objections to the body being handled by non-Hindu, although there can be many variations on the theme because of the diversity of the religion. The Asian Funeral Service arranges Hindu funerals and organises repatriation for those who require a funeral by the Ganges.

Sikh funerals

Sikhism has a lot in common with Hinduism but there is a strong emphasis on militarism.

There are five symbols of faith important to the Sikh. The Kesh is the uncut hair, which, for men, is always turbaned. The Kangha is a ritual comb, which keeps the hair in place and is never removed. The Kara is a steel bracelet worn on the right wrist. The Kirpan is a small symbolic dagger. The Kaccha are ceremonial undergarments, which are never completely removed even when bathing. Sikhs are always cremated and never buried. The family will always insist that their dead are buried with all five K symbols.

After a death, men are dressed in a white cotton shroud and turban, older women in white and young women in red. Cremation will usually take place within 24 hours. The coffin will usually be taken home before cremation for last respects to be paid. The oldest son will press the crematoria button or see the coffin into the cremator. Ashes are scattered in a river or in the sea or taken back for scattering in the Punjab in India.

Buddhist funerals

After death, Buddhists will prepare a person for death and wrap the body in a plain sheet. There are differing customs within Buddhism, as it is a very diverse religion.

Jewish funerals

Orthodox Jews are very strict when it comes to funerals while more progressive Jews have differing attitudes. When a Jewish person dies, the body is traditionally left for eight minutes while a feather is placed in the mouth or nostrils to detect signs of breathing. Eyes and mouth are then closed by the eldest son, or the nearest relative. Many Jews appoint "watchers" this being a person or people who will stay with the body day or night until the funeral, praying and reciting.

The dead are buried as soon as possible. Cremation is not accepted by the Orthodox Jew. Orthodox Rabbis will sometimes permit the burial of cremated remains in a full size coffin, and say Kaddish (prayer) for the deceased. Jewish funerals are usually arranged by a Jewish funeral agency. Otherwise, the local Jewish community will arrange a contract with a gentile Funeral Director, but under strict Rabbinical control. The Jewish Counseling Service offers support to those who have lost another. See useful addresses at the back of the book.

Cult funerals

There are an enormous number of different Christian cults in the U.K., including Mormons and Jehovah's Witnesses, Christian Scientists, Scientologists, Moonies and the Children of God. For most there is little or no deviation from orthodox Christian practice.

Some groups became prominent in the 1960's, such as Hare Krishna and will normally adopt Hindu practices.

Now read the key points from chapter four.

Key points from chapter four

- Great Britain is a multi-racial society and it is important that those who reside here show sensitivity to the customs of other cultures as they apply to groups in the U.K.

5

After a Funeral is Over

When a funeral service is finished, there is usually a gathering of family and friends at the house of the deceased, or at a venue organized by relatives. The organising of this event is important as mourners need to be clearly informed about what has been arranged and where it is being held.

The funeral director will submit an account, which is usually very detailed and will require payment within a reasonable amount of time. If the money is from the estate, there should be no problem arranging for the release of the funds to pay for a funeral. Legally, payment of the funeral bill is the first claim on the estate of the deceased, taking priority over income tax and any other claims.

Memorials

Relatives of the deceased often want to place a memorial tablet or headstone in a churchyard or cemetery where the person is buried. There are normally restrictions on the size of the memorial and full details of the restrictions can be obtained from the burial ground.

The funeral director or monumental mason will normally apply to the church or cemetery authorities for permission to erect a memorial. After a burial, several months should be allowed for settlement before any memorial is erected or replaced. Time and consideration should be given to a memorial, and names of Burial Authorities. The cost of memorial will vary enormously, depending on what has been purchased and a written estimate should be obtained before any order is given.

After cremation

About one week after cremation has taken place, the crematorium will usually send a brochure to the next of kin explaining what kinds of memorials are available. These are all optional and are not covered by the fees paid for the cremation.

The most popular means of memorial at the cremation is the book of remembrance. Hand lettered inscriptions in the book usually consist of the name, date of death, and a short epitaph. The charge depends on the length of entry.

The crematorium displays the book, open at the right page, on the anniversary of the funeral. The crematoria will provide a list of charges on request.

Some crematoria have a colonnade of niches for ashes called a columbarium. The ashes are either walled in by a plaque or left in an urn by the niche. Charges for this are high, where space can be found. In addition to the above, some crematoria have memorial trees, or rose bushes. These are usually arranged in beds, where the memorial bush is chosen by the family, the ashes are scattered around it, and a small plaque placed nearby. Costs vary and can be provided by the crematoria in question.

Ashes generally

Once a cremation is over, if you want you can get the ashes back. There are a number of things that you can do with the ashes. You can bury them in your local cemetery or in a natural burial ground. You can scatter them. You can divide them up amongst members of the family. You can get the crematorium to scatter them. There are many things that can be done with the ashes.

Here are a few suggestions

- Keep the ashes in an urn, this is a very common way of dealing with the ashes

- Mix them in clay or some other material and make something with them

- Scatter them from a hot air balloon or aircraft
- Scatter them at sea

- Have them turned into a diamond-go to phoenix-diamonds.com

- Have them mixed with glass and made into an ornament or pendant. Go to ashesintoglass.co.uk

- Keep them in a locket, ring or pendant. Go to urns-coffins-caskets.co.uk

- Have them made into a firework display. Go to heavensabovefireworks.com

- Fire them into space. Go to heavensabovefireworks.com

These are just a few options for you to think about.

Charitable donations

An increasing number of people will request that family and friends make a charitable donation to a nominated charity in memory of the deceased and will regard this as a fitting memorial for the person concerned. Usually, the funeral director will arrange to collect and forward donations and will not charge for this service.

6

The Estate of the Deceased-Applying for Probate

Probate simply means that the executor's powers to administer the estate of a dead person have been officially confirmed. A document called a "Grant of Representation" is given which enables those administering the estate to gain access to all relevant information, financial or otherwise concerning the person's estate.

Although anyone charged under a will to act on behalf of the dead persons estate has automatic authority to represent, there are certain cases where evidence of probate is required. If no will exists or no executors have been appointed, then it will be necessary to obtain "letters of administration" which involves a similar procedure. Under common law, probate has a number of objectives. These are:

- To safeguard creditors of the deceased

- To ensure reasonable provision is made for the deceased's dependants

- To distribute the balance of the estate in accordance with the intentions of the person whose will it is.

One of the key factors affecting the need to obtain probate is how much money is involved under the terms of a will. Where the sums involved are relatively small then financial institutions and other organisations will not normally want to see evidence of probate. However, it should be remembered that no one is obliged to release anything relating to a dead person's estate unless letters of administration or documents of probate can be shown. Those responsible for administering the estate must find out from the organisations concerned what the necessary procedure is.

Applying for probate

Where a will is in existence and executors have been appointed then any one of the named people can make the application. Where a will is in existence but no executors have been appointed, then the person who benefits from the whole estate should make the application. This would be the case where any known executor cannot or will not apply for probate. Where there is no will in existence then the next of kin can apply for probate. There is an order of priority relating to the application:

- The surviving spouse

- A child of the deceased

- A parent of the deceased

- A brother or sister of the deceased

- Another relative of the deceased

The person applying for probate must be over eighteen. Children includes any that are illegitimate. If a child dies before the deceased then one of his or her children can apply for probate.

Making the application

This can be done through any probate registry or office. There is usually one in every main town and any office in any area will accept the application. If you are writing then you should always address your correspondence to a registry and not an office.

What needs to be done next?

The next of kin should register the death with the Register of Births and Deaths. A death certificate will be supplied and copies of the death certificate, which will need to be included to various institutions and organisations. A copy of the will has to be obtained. The whereabouts should be known to the executors. The executor should then take a copy of the will in case the original is lost. The executor will need to obtain full details of the dead person's estate, including all property and other items together with a current valuation. It is possible that on many of the less substantial items a personal valuation can be made. It should however, be as accurate as possible.

In the case of any bank accounts a letter should be sent by the executor to the bank manager, stating that he/she is the executor and giving full details of the death. Details should be requested concerning the amount of money in the dead person's account(s) together with any other details of valuables lodged with the bank.

The bank manager may be able to pass on information concerning holdings in stocks and shares. If share certificates are held then a valuation of the shares at time of death should be requested.

In the case of insurance policies, the same procedure should be followed. A letter should be sent to the insurance company requesting details of policies and amounts owed or payable.

In the case of National Savings Certificates the executor should write to the Savings Certificate Office in Durham and ask for a list of all certificates held, date of issue and current value. In the case of Premium Bonds a letter should be sent to National Savings and Investments, Glasgow G58 1SB giving name and date of death. Premium Bonds remain in the draw for 12 months after death, so they can be left invested for that time or cashed in when probate has been obtained. Form SB4 (obtained from any post office) is used to inform of death and obtain repayment of most government bonds.

In the case of property, whatever valuation is put on a property HM Revenues and Customs can always insist on its own valuation. If there is a mortgage, the executor should write to the mortgagee asking for the amount outstanding at the time of death.

The above procedure should be followed when writing to any one or an organisation, such as a pension fund, requesting details of monies owed to the dead person.

Debts owed by the person

The executor will need to compile a list of debts owed by the dead person as these will need to be paid out of the estate. These debts will include all money owed, loans, overdrafts, bills and other liabilities. If there is any doubt about the extent of the debts then the executor can advertise in the London Gazette and any newspaper, which circulates in the area where the estate is situated. Efforts also have to be made to locate creditors outside of advertising. The advert will tell creditors that they have to claim by a certain date after which the estate will be administered having obtained probate. Funeral expenses should be quantified and a letter should be sent to HMRC to determine the income tax position of the dead person. The executor obtains the application form, decide where he or she wishes to be interviewed, send the completed form together with the death certificate and the original will to the Probate Registry and then attend for an interview.

The forms

The forms consist of the following:

Form PR1-Probate Application form

Form IHT 205 short form where inheritance tax not due

Form IHT 200 long form where tax due
There will be instructions on application as to how to fill these forms in. It may be possible for an interview to take place on the same day as the forms are received by the appropriate office. The forms can be delivered either personally or by post.

The interview

The interview is to iron out any problems with the application and to get the executor to swear or affirm before the Probate Officer that the information in the forms is true (to the best of knowledge). The taxation form for inheritance purposes has to be signed so that it can be returned to HMRC for assessment. Probate fees have to be paid at the interview. These are worked out on the value of the net estate. A list of current fees can be obtained from any Probate Office. After the interview the Probate Registry will send the account of the estate to the capital taxes office for an assessment of any inheritance tax payable. Once the Probate Registry has received an assessment then this will be sent to the executor who should then make arrangements for payment.

The tax should be paid before Probate is granted or letters of administration are given. It must be paid within six months of the date of death.

After a few weeks, the executor will receive grant of Probate. This is simply a sheet of paper which details that the dead person, of a particular address died on a particular day and that the executor has been granted the administration of the estate. The gross and net value at a specific date are stated. Attached is the probate copy of the will. The executor receives the original death certificate. All probate documents become public property which are open for inspection by the public. Further copies of probate documents can be obtained for a fee.

Now read the key points from Chapter six

Key points from Chapter six

- Probate means that the executor's powers to administer the estate of the dead person have been officially confirmed

- Probate has a number of objectives under the law-to safeguard the creditors of the deceased, to ensure reasonable provision is made for the deceased's dependants and to distribute the balance of the estate in accordance with the intentions of the person whose will it is

- One of the key factors affecting the need to obtain probate is how much money is left under the will

7

The Intervention of the Courts

Courts have wide powers to make alterations to a persons will, after that person's death. It can exercise these powers if the will fails to achieve the intentions of the person who wrote it, as a result of a clerical error or a failure to understand the instructions of the person producing the will. In addition, if mental illness can be demonstrated at the time of producing the will then this can also lead to the courts intervening.

In order to get the courts to exercise their powers, an application must be made within six months of the date on which probate is taken out. If gifts or other are distributed and a court order is made to rectify the will then all must be returned to be distributed in accordance with the court order.

If any part of a persons will appears to have no meaning or is ambiguous then the court will look at any surrounding evidence and the testators intention and will rectify the will in the light of this evidence.

The right to dispose of property

In general, the law allows an unfettered right to dispose of a persons property as they choose. This however is subject to tax and the courts powers to intervene. The law has been consolidated in the Inheritance (Provision for Family and Dependants Act) 1975. In addition, The Civil Partnerships Act of 2004 now grants powers to civil partners. Certain categories of people can now apply to the court and be given money out of a deceased person's will. This can be done whether there is a will or not.

The husband or wife or civil partner of a deceased person can be given any amount of money as the court thinks reasonable. The 1975 Act implemented the recommendations of the Law Commission that felt that a surviving spouse should be given money out of an estate on the same principles as a spouse is given money when there is a divorce. This means that, even if a will is not made, or there are inadequate provisions then a surviving spouse can make an application to rectify the situation.

The situation is different for other relations. They can apply to the court to have a will rectified but will receive far less than the spouse. The following can claim against a will:

- The wife or husband or civil partner of the deceased

- A former wife or former husband/civil partner of the deceased who has not remarried

- A child of the deceased

- Any person who is not included as a child of the deceased but who was treated by the deceased as a child of the family in relation to any marriage during his lifetime

- Any other person who was being maintained, even if only partly maintained, by the deceased just before his or her death

Former spouse/civil partner

There is one main condition under which a former spouse can claim and that is that they have not remarried. In addition, such a claim would be for only essential maintenance that would stop on remarriage. There is one key exception, that is that if your death occurs within a year of divorce or legal separation, your former spouse can make a claim.

Child of the deceased

As the above, any claim by children can only be on the basis of hardship.

Stepchildren

This includes anyone treated as your own child and supported by you, including illegitimate children or those conceived before, but not born till after, your death. The claim can only cover essential maintenance.

Dependants

This covers a wide range of potential claimants. Maintenance only is payable. There needs to be evidence of full or partial maintenance prior to death. Such support does not have to be financial, however.

There is another situation where the court can change a will after your death. This relates directly to conditions that you may have imposed on a beneficiary in order to receive a gift that are unreasonable. If the court decides that this is the case, that particular condition becomes void and does not have to be fulfilled.

If the condition involved something being done before the beneficiary receives the gift then the beneficiary does not receive the gift. If the condition involved something being done after the beneficiary received the gift then the beneficiary can have the gift without condition.

If the beneficiary does not receive the gift, as in the above, then either the will can make alternative provision or the gift can form part of the residue of the estate.

Unreasonable conditions can be many, one such being any condition that provides reason or incentive to break up a marriage, intention to remain celibate or not to remarry or one that separates children.

There are others that impinge on religion, general behaviour and crime. An unreasonable condition very much depends on the perception of the beneficiary and the perception of the courts.

A beneficiary can lose the right to a bequest, apart from any failure to meet conditions attached to a bequest. Again, a court will decide in what circumstance this is appropriate. Crime could be a reason, such as murder, or evidence of coercion or harassment of another person in pursuit of selfish gain.

8

Welfare Benefits after Death

After the death of a spouse, you may be entitled to a number of benefits from the state. The Department of Work and Pensions, through its agency Jobcentre Plus administers all social security benefits and explanatory leaflets are available.

Some of the benefits available are paid only to those dependants of people who had paid, or had credited to them, National Insurance Contributions during their lifetime. The number of contributions required varies according to the type of benefit. Reduced rates are paid in certain circumstances.

Benefits can be paid after someone has died abroad. Write to the Overseas Branch of the Department of Social Security.

The figures below are at 2010/11 levels.

Funeral payments

If you or your partner (a person you are married to, or person you live with as if you are married to them or a civil partner, or person you live with as if you were civil partners) together, are getting

Income Support, Income Based Jobseeker's allowance, Income Related Employment and Support Allowance, Pension Credit, Working Families Tax Credit which includes a disability or severe disability element, Child Tax Credit at a rate higher than the family element, Council Tax Benefit or Housing Benefit, you may be able to get assistance with the funeral costs if it is seen as reasonable that you should bear responsibility for the funeral and associated costs.

You must claim a funeral payment from the date of death and up to three months after the date of the funeral. If you get a funeral payment it must be paid back from the estate of the person who died. A house or personal things that are left to a widow, widower or surviving civil partner will not be counted as part of the estate.

Relationship with the person who has died

To be able to get a funeral payment you must also be either:

- The partner of the deceased when they died

- The parent of the deceased child, or have been responsible for the deceased child (and there is no absent parent) (unless they are getting one of the above qualifying benefits or were estranged from the child at the date of death)
- The parent of a still born child

- A close relative or close friend of the deceased (and it is reasonable for you to accept responsibility for the funeral costs).

Who isn't eligible?

You can't get a payment as a close relative or close friend of the deceased if either:

- The deceased had a partner when they died
- There is a parent, son or daughter of the deceased who has not been awarded one of the qualifying benefits or was not estranged from the deceased. This doesn't include family members who are: aged under 18, qualifying young persons for the purposes of child benefit, full-time students, members of religious orders, in prison or in hospital (and who had been awarded a qualifying benefit immediately before they entered prison or hospital) asylum seekers being supported by the National Asylum Support Service or family members not ordinarily resident in the UK
- There is a close relative of the deceased, other than a close relative in one of the excluded groups listed above, who was in closer contact with the deceased than you were, or had equally close contact and is not getting a qualifying benefit.

The Social Fund will, subject to certain criteria, meet specified costs, including burial and cremation costs plus up to £700 for other funeral costs. It has to be borne in mind that the social fund will not pay for anything other than the essential costs, these do not include items such as newspaper insertions or any other costs such as flowers and so on.

Other sources of funding such as life insurance policies, are also taken into account. The Social Fund Allowance is not treated as a loan as such, but is repayable from the deceased person's estate if there is money to do so. Claims should be made on form SF200 available from Job center Plus or the funeral directors and must be sent in with a copy of the funeral directors account. Your local Social Security office will supply you with the address of the relevant office to forward the form to. It is most important to check with the Department of Social Security concerning the range and types of benefits available and also the amounts.

Bereavement allowance

This is a regular payment, paid for 52 weeks from the bereavement and based on the late husband or wife's or civil partner's National insurance contributions.

Who can claim?

You may be able to claim bereavement allowance if all of the following applies:

- You are a widow, widower or surviving civil partner aged

45 or over when you husband, wife or civil partner died
- You are not bringing up children
- You are under state pension age (currently 60 for women and 65 for men)
- Your late husband, wife or civil partner paid National Insurance contributions or they died as a result of an industrial accident or disease

Who can't claim?

You can't claim bereavement allowance if:

- You were divorced from your late husband or wife at the time of their death
- Your civil partnership was dissolved at the time of your civil partner's death
- You are living with another person as if you are married to them or as if you have formed a civil partnership
- You are in prison

If you were over state pension age when you were widowed or became a surviving civil partner you may get extra state pension based on your late husband's, wife's or civil partners NICs.

If you are widowed below state pension age and you have a dependant child you can claim widowed parent's allowance. You cannot get widowed parents allowance and bereavement allowance at the same time.

There are a range of payments £97.65 at age 55 to state pension age. The actual amount that you might receive depends on:

- The overall level of your partner or civil partner's National insurance contributions
- Your age at the time of his or her death
- If relevant, when your Widowed Parent's Allowance stops, and this is within 52 weeks of your bereavement, you may be able to get bereavement allowance. This will depend on your age at the time you were bereaved.

How to claim

If you are of state pension age when your spouse or partner/civil partner dies then you will automatically get the bereavement payment when you notify DWP of the death. In other cases, you can order a Bereavement Benefits Claim pack, Form BB1 over the telephone from your nearest jobcentre plus or social security office. You can also download a form from the Department of Works and pensions (DWP) website dwp.gov.uk

Bereavement payment

A Bereavement payment is a one off lump sum based on the late husbands or wife's or civil partner's national insurance contributions which is £2000 if National Insurance Contributions were up to date or their death was caused by their job and either:

- You were under State pension Age (currently 60 for women and 65 for men although changing) when they died

Or

- Your husband, wife or civil partner was not entitled to a category A State Retirement Benefit when they died.

Who can't claim?

You can't get bereavement payment if any of the following apply:

- You were divorced from your late husband or wife or the civil partnership had dissolved at the time of the civil partner's death
- You are living with another person as husband, wife or civil partner
- You are in prison

Crisis loans

Crisis loans can sometimes be applicable to those who have suffered bereavement and it is worth outlining criteria for these loans.

If you need financial help with an emergency or disaster, you may be able to get a crisis loan, which is an interest free loan from the social fund that you have to pay back.

Who is eligible?

You can apply for a crisis loan if all the following apply:

- You are aged 16 or over
- You don't have enough money to meet your or your family's immediate short term needs in an emergency or as a result of a disaster
- Without the loan there will be a serious damage or risk to your or your family's health or safety

Or if all the following apply

You are aged 16 or over and you have:

- been getting a Community Care Grant but you are moving out of institutional or residential accommodation and don't have enough money to pay advance rent to a non-local authority landlord.

There is no set amount of crisis loan this will vary according to circumstances.

War widow's or widowers pensions

A War Widow's or Widower's pension is a tax-free pension you may be entitled to if your wife, husband or civil partner died as a result of their service in Her majesty's Armed Forces or at time of war.

Who is eligible?

You may be entitled to a War Widow's pension or Widower's Pension if any of the following apply:

Your husband, wife or civil partner:

- Died as a result of their service in HM Armed Forces before April 6th 2005

- Was a civil defence volunteer or a civilian and their death was a result of the 1939-45 war

- Was a merchant seaman, a member of the naval auxiliary services or a coastguard and their death was a result of an injury or disease they got during a war or because they were a prisoner of war

- Died as a result of their service as a member of the Polish forces under British command during the 1939 to 1945 war, or in the polish resettlement forces

- Was getting a war pensions Constant Attendance Allowance at the time of their death, or would have been had they not been in hospital

- Was getting a War Disablement Pension at the 80 per cent rate or higher and was getting unemployability Supplement.

For those who served after 6th April 2005, The Armed forces Compensation Scheme offers financial help.

Unmarried partners

You may be entitled to a pension if you lived with your partner or civil partner as husband or wife.

How much do I get?

War Widow's pension is paid at the higher rate if you are:

- The widow, widower or surviving civil partner of an office above the rank of major or equivalent

- Aged 40 or over

- Aged under 40 and getting an allowance for a child and unable to support yourself financially

Otherwise, you will get the lower rate of pension until you reach 40 when you will get the higher rate pension.

Additional allowances

You may get additional allowance if:

- You have children

- You have accommodation costs (this only applies if you are getting an allowance for a child with a war Widow's or Widower's pension)

- You are aged over 65, 70 or 80

- Your husband, wife or civil partner was discharged from the armed forces before march 31st 1973

Temporary allowance for Widows or Widowers

You may get this allowance for 26 weeks after your wife, husband or civil partner has died if they were getting War Pensions Constant Attendance Allowance Unemployability Supplement or your partner/civil partner was entitled to unemployability supplement that wasn't paid because they chose to continue getting Allowance for Lowered Satndard of Occupation.

Funeral expenses

The Service Personnel and Veterans Agency may be able to pay a maximum of £1400 towards a simple funeral to a widow or widower, next of kin of person paying for the funeral if:

- Death was due to service before 6th April 2005

- War Pensions Constant Attendance Allowance was being paid or would have been paid if the war pensioner had not been in hospital when they died

- Unemployability Supplement was being paid at the time of death and the War Disablement Pension was assessed at 80% or more

Or

- The person died in hospital while having treatment for a disablement they were getting a war disablement pension for.

You must make a claim within three months of the funeral.

You can check current rates of benefit by obtaining the Service Personnel leaflet: rates of War Pension and Allowances 2010/11

Widowed Parents Allowance

If you are a parent whose husband, wife or civil partner has died and you have a dependant child or young person (aged 16 and under 20) for whom you receive child benefit, you may be able to get Widowed parent Allowance (WPA).

Who can claim?

You may get WPA if all the following apply:
- You are bringing up a child or young person under 19 (or under 20 in some cases) for whom you are getting child benefit.

- You are under State Pension Age (60 for women and 65 for men)

- Your husband, wife or civil partner died

- Your husband, wife or civil partner paid National insurance Contributions (NIC).

You may also claim WPA:

- If you are expecting your late husband's baby or your late civil partners baby (with whom you were pregnant from fertility treatment)

- Your husband, wife or civil partner died as a result of their work-even if they didn't pay NICs

Who can't claim?

You can't claim if:

- You were divorced from your husband or wife or the civil partnership had dissolved when the civil partner died

- You remarry or are living with a partner as husband and wife or as if you had formed a civil partnership

- You are in prison

How much can you claim?

£95.25 per week (2010/11) is the maximum basic allowance of Widowed Parent's Allowance. There may be an entitlement to an additional pension.

State Second Pension (previously SERPS)

In addition to the standard Widows Pension, a woman may also receive and additional pension based on her husband's earnings as an employed person from April 1978. This pension will be worked out according to a sliding scale revised annually. If her husband was a member of a contracted out occupational pension scheme, part of the widow's additional pension will be paid by that scheme.

A widow can inherit the whole of her late husbands basic and State Second Pension. If she is entitled to a retirement pension based on her own contributions, she can add the two Retirement Pensions together.

A man whose wife dies when they are both over retirement age can draw a pension derived partly from her contribution record and partly from his own, in exactly the same way that a widow can do, up to the same maximum.

A woman who is not yet drawing Retirement Pension when her husband dies may qualify for a widows pension, even if she goes on working. Once she has retired, or reached the age of 65, she may inherit half her husbands graduated pension to add to her Retirement Pension as well as any graduated pension of her own. For more information on this you should go the to DWP website.

Other state benefits

A widow whose income and savings are below certain defined levels may be able to claim benefits to top up her income. Advice can be obtained from the Benefits Agency or from Citizens Advice Bureau.

Other benefits, which can be obtained, are:

Income support-a widow who works less than 16 hours per week and has less than £16000 savings can claim income support if her weekly income is below a certain amount

Working Tax Credit-a widow who works for 16 hours per week or more, has dependent children and has savings of less than £8000 can apply for Working Family tax Credit if her weekly income is below a certain amount

Housing Benefit-a widow whose savings are below £16000 may be able to claim Housing Benefit to help her pay her rent and council tax if her income is below a certain amount, which varies according to circumstances

Industrial Injuries Disablement Benefit-if a widow's husband did not meet or fully meet NI contributions conditions, they may be treated as satisfied if the death was as a result of industrial injury, accident or disease. Jobseeker's allowance-a widow who is unemployed and able to look for work may be eligible to receive jobseeker's allowance

Orphans-a person who takes an orphaned child into a family may be entitled to a guardian's allowance. It is not necessary to be a legal guardian to apply. There are various criteria dealing with this which should be verified with the DSS.

Home Responsibilities Protection-a widow who is looking after a child or a sick or disabled person, and either does not work at all or works but does not pay enough NI Contributions in a tax year to make that count for Retirement Pension Purposes may benefit from home responsibilities protection. This is a special arrangement to protect basic retirement pensions.

Information concerning all of the above may be obtained from Jobcentre plus. Please check the amounts quoted as these are for guidance only.

Useful Addresses

There are a number of agencies that provide help to those who have experienced bereavement. Below is a list of the key agencies with addresses, phone numbers and in most cases e mails.

Age Concern
England
Astral House 1268 London Road
Norbury
London SW16 4ER
Tel: 0208 765 7200
E mail contact:@ageuk.org.uk

Scotland
Causeway House
160 Causewayside
Edinburgh EH9 1PR
Tel: 0845 1259732
enquiries@ageconcernandhelptheagescotland.org.uk

Northern Ireland
3 Lower Crescent
Belfast BT7 1NR
0208 9204 5792
info@ageni.org

Wales
13/14 Neptune Court
Vanguard Way
Cardiff CF24 5PJ
Tel: 029 2043 1555
enquiries@agecymru.org.uk

Asian Funeral Service
209 Kenton road
Harrow
Middlesex HA3 OHD
Tel: 0208 909 3737

Association of Burial Authorities
Waterloo House
155 Upper Street
London N1 1RD
Tel: 0207 288 2522
Fax: 0207 288 2533
Email aba@burials.org.uk

British Organ Donors Society
(Body)
Balsham, Cambridge CB1 6DL
Tel/Fax 01223 893636
Email body@argonet.uk

Cremation Society
1st Floor, Brecon House
16-16a Albion Place
Maidstone ME14 5DZ
Tel: 01622 688292/3
Fax: 01622 686698
info@cremation.org.uk

Cruse-Bereavement Care
1 Princes Street
Richmond, TW9 1UR
Tel: 0208 876 0147
info@cruserichmonduponthames.org.uk

Foundation for the Study of Infant Death
11 Belgrave Road
London SW1V 1RB
Tel: 0207 802 3200
office@frid.co.uk

Funeral Ombudsman Scheme
26-28 Bedford Row
London WC1R 4HE
Tel: 0207 430 1112
fos@dircon.co.uk

Funeral Planning Authority
Knellstone House
Udimore
Rye
East Sussex
TN31 6AR
0845 601 9619

Inquest
89/93 Fonthill Road
London N4 3JH
0208 263 1111

Institute of Family Therapy
24-32 Stephenson Way
London NW1 2HX
Tel: 0207 391 9150
Fax: 0207 391 9169

Jewish Bereavement Counseling Service
Beit Meir
44 Albert Road
Hendon
London NW4 2SG
Tel 0208 457 9710

Lesbian and Gay Bereavement Project
86 Caledonian Road
London N1 9DN
General enquiries 0208 7833 1674
Helpline 020 7403 5699

National Association of Funeral Directors
618 Warwick Road
Solihull
West Midlands B91 1AA
Tel: 0121 711 1343
Fax: 0121 711 1351

National Association of Memorial Masons
1 Castle Mews
Rugby, CV21 2XL
Tel: 01788 542 264
Fax: 01788 542 276

National Association of Pre-Paid Funeral Plans
15 Riverside Drive
Solihull
West Midlands B91 3HH
Tel: 0121 705 5133
burtonnr@btinternet.com

National Association of Widows
3rd Floor 48 Queens Road
Coventry CV1 3EH
Tel: 0845 839 2261
info@nawidows.org.uk

Society of Allied and Independent Funeral Directors
SAIF Business Centre
3 Bullfields
Sawbridgeworth
Herts
CM21 9DD
0845 230 6777

Index

www.straightforwardco.co.uk

In addition to Easyway Guides, all titles, listed below, in the Straightforward Guides Series can be purchased online, using credit card or other forms of payment by going to www.straightfowardco.co.uk A discount of 25% per title is offered with online purchases.

Law
A Straightforward Guide to:
Consumer Rights
Bankruptcy Insolvency and the Law
Employment Law
Private Tenants Rights
Family law
Small Claims in the County Court
Contract law
Intellectual Property and the law
Divorce and the law
Leaseholders Rights
The Process of Conveyancing
Knowing Your Rights and Using the Courts
Producing Your own Will
Housing Rights
The Bailiff the law and You
Probate and The Law
Company law

What to Expect When You Go to Court
Guide to Competition Law
Give me Your Money-Guide to Effective Debt Collection
Caring for a Disabled Child

General titles
Letting Property for Profit
Buying, Selling and Renting property
Buying a Home in England and France
Bookkeeping and Accounts for Small Business
Creative Writing
Freelance Writing
Writing Your own Life Story
Writing performance Poetry
Writing Romantic Fiction
Speech Writing
Writing Perfect Essays
Teaching Your Child to Read and write
Teaching Your Child to Swim
Raising a Child-The Early Years
Creating a Successful Commercial Website
The Straightforward Business Plan
The Straightforward C.V.
Successful Public Speaking
Play the Game-A Compendium of Rules
Individual and Personal Finance
Understanding Mental Illness
The Two-Minute Message

Guide to Self Defence
Buying a Used Car
Tiling for Beginners
Guide to The Stock Market

Go to:

www.straightforwardco.co.uk